CU00950205

Being a Zebra

My Story of Being a Christian with Chronic Illness and Depression

By Alise Gilley

I'm writing this book, not to get sympathy or to shine light on me. I am writing this book for those of you who battle with your body. I want to encourage you to keep pushing until you get answers. I also want to encourage you to seek out a good, solid support system. I also am writing this book for all the people who love and support someone with a chronic illness. The final hope I have for this book is that my story helps to break the stigma around mental illness, especially in Christian communities.

Chapter One

Betrayed by My Own Body

I grew up in a Christian family. I had a loving mom and dad. My dad worked very hard to provide for my family and my mom stayed home to raise and care for my two sisters and me. I had all the ingredients needed to be a happy, healthy, successful Christian woman. Christ drew me to Him when I was only a child, and I have always been sensitive to Him and His spirit.

My story of salvation is simple. I didn't do drugs or wander way off the straight and narrow. I simply had diligent parents who kept me exposed to the gospel every chance they had. We talked about it in the home, we went to church and I even went to Bible School. God used these conditions to soften my heart and pull me to Him, until I made the relationship I saw in my parents my own. Christ was and is truly the centerpiece of my life.

I was confused in sixth grade when I started to experience pain in my ankle. I wasn't particularly athletic or rambunctious. I had just gotten a flu bug and when it was time to go back to school, it hurt terribly bad to walk on that foot. Of course, there was no swelling, and no injury to make my mom believe that I was injured, so she made me go to school. Before you think my mom was some tyrant, you must realize, all my friends were playing basketball this year and a couple of them were on crutches. Mom thought that I wanted to be like them, so I was playing up a pain. I remember the walk up to the school very well. Our elementary school had a small parking lot that the school buses used. Behind that was a church with a large parking lot. We always parked in the church parking lot then walked across. It hurt so bad to walk and Mom could tell I was not faking. I don't believe I even made it into the school before Mom decided it was time to go to the doctor.

I went to the doctor, and he felt around my ankle. He bent my foot around and there was still no swelling. He could tell I was in pain, but there was no real factor that made him think there was something majorly wrong. Since I had the flu the week before, he thought maybe the flu had flared up some type of juvenile arthritis. He just told Mom to give me some over the counter pain relief meds and give it some extra support. This seemed to make sense. I was at the age where my body chemistry was changing so why would I doubt the man with a medical degree. After a little while of taking Tylenol and wearing high top shoes, (thank goodness it was the 90's and they were in style) they began to make my ankle feel better. So, we didn't give it too much extra thought.

The summer between my seventh and eighth grade year I decided to give softball a try. The girls in my youth group played on the church softball team and they said that they that they would show me how to play. I picked up the game quickly. It was slow pitch softball, so nothing too intense.

I made the team, not by my talent, but simply because everyone did. I wasn't an all-star player, so I was placed in the two spots that risked our team's success the least. I played outfield and catcher. Most of my time I played at catcher. I would throw the ball back to the pitcher a lot, and I found that near the end of the season, I was having trouble throwing the ball. My once straight throw was now getting erratic and my shoulder was starting to hurt. I also found that my hips and knees were really getting painful from squatting and standing. Then there was of course the intense pain of the follow-thru from swinging the bat. I figured this was normal since I hadn't played too many sports.

It became evident that this was not normal when my arm began to pop. I would try to lift my arm over my head to get a cup or something from the cupboard and it would have to pop before I could move it all the way up. When I say pop, I don't mean a sound. I mean like a sickening pop you could not only hear, but visibly see. It sort of reminded me of a train jumping the tracks. It was becoming very painful. I was keeping ice on it and taking a large amount of ibuprofen and avoiding motions and activities that aggravated my shoulder. I was feeling rather blue and exhausted. Being emotional and tired seemed like a natural thing for a girl my age especially with the tremendous amount of pain I was always in.

Mom finally trumped my resistance to go to the doctor and made me go in. When I saw my regular family doctor, he found that my shoulder was out of joint. this was not a simple dislocation. It was loosely hanging out of joint. This explained the popping. My shoulder was popping in and out of joint as I changed the position. This was not something he would commonly expect to see, especially since there was no injury that caused this. He decided it would be good for me to see an orthopedic doctor and get another opinion on what to do for treatment. At this point he wasn't sure if surgery was the answer or if it should be physical therapy. I was very opposed to surgery so I was hoping for the physical therapy option.

Thankfully, my orthopedic doctor felt the same way. Shoulder surgery tends to be very complex and due to my age, the type of surgery that would be recommended would not be beneficial. The surgery would essentially have been attempting to shorten the ligaments that hold my shoulder in place. This is by putting a stitch in them and letting the scar tissue do the rest. I was still growing, and I was obviously opposed to surgery, so physical therapy was the answer.

I was sent to a great therapist who knew how to motivate me. I remember the first time I met him. I was feeling particularly blue. I had on a little fake leather jacket and camouflage pants, on my five-foot two-inch 95 pound body, and a dog collar to drive home the fact that I was pretty much bad to the bone. I was really down and out. The list of things I couldn't do was growing. I was very focused on this list and was starting to believe it wasn't going to get any better. I remember my therapist looking at me and saying, "Well, I guess we better call the nursing home and get you a bed." This made me just angry enough that I wanted to show him I could get better.

Once my therapist saw a little grit in my personality, he knew it was time to get to work. I am not a touchy person at all. I like my personal space a lot. However, I was an oddity. My shoulder had stretched, not torn, but stretched. The therapist could put three fingers between my shoulder and the bone in my arm. Apparently, if you are in the medical field, this is way cool to see. Not so much if you're the one who is the oddity. All the therapists in the office flocked to check out my shoulder. I was surrounded by strangers poking and prodding me while I stood there in pain wearing nothing but a bra.

The first thing that the therapist wanted to try was taping my shoulder into place. It took two people and they held my shoulder where it belonged. With the tape holding my arm where it should be, I could use it again with little pain. It was amazing, until my skin started to react to the tape. The redness was spreading very quickly, the therapist and his help were trying to get the tape off as quickly as they could before it damaged my skin too much. It took several days for the redness and tenderness to go away. So obviously, tape was not going to be an option. We were back to square one. There was no immediate fix for my issues. It was going to be the slow process of strength training. For the next several months after this, I worked on getting strong. They taught me how to build the muscles up to compensate for what the ligaments were not going to do. It was a lot of work but it gave me back my mobility. I was told if I kept up that work out regularly, I would be able to play softball again and do pretty much whatever I wanted.

This was short lived once the next softball season came around. I found myself back at the doctor and back in therapy. We found that it was more than just my shoulders. The pain became widespread. The fatigue became overwhelming and all my joints became undependable. Even my pinky finger would dislocate when I played my clarinet. I was very frustrated. It was my freshman year, and my emotions were erratic to say the least.

I remember getting frustrated or scared about something and getting into arguments with my dad. The arguments would always be so circular. I would always come back to the same thing, like I was stuck. There was no reasoning, no calming, it always just ended with lots of tears and both parties going away frustrated. We chocked this up as a hormonal teenage girl.

I began missing a lot of school. It seemed any time I would get a cold or the flu it would turn into something bigger. I had the ear infection that swelled my ear shut. Pneumonia and at least one bout of bronchitis happened every year. I required a lot of sleep. I would sleep any time I could. I was pretty much able to go to school and do my homework but everything else went to the wayside so I could get rest.

I did some research on the internet to see if I could find anything like I had. Anyone else who had ligaments that stretched. I did find an online support group for a condition called Elhers Danlos syndrome. I didn't have the stretchy skin, so I thought I obviously couldn't have that, but I did have the many injuries and stretching ligaments. Even though I didn't fit this profile exactly, I still joined in on the conversation in the forum. I met two girls that I chatted with over email for a few years. It was tremendously helpful to have someone to talk to that had some idea of what it was like to have the struggle. It also gave me someone to talk to that didn't feel sorry for me or have tons of questions. When I talked to them I could feel a sense of normalcy.

In this trying time, I was building my support system. In addition to my two friends I was emailing and my family, my boyfriend became a great support. My boyfriend would always be there along with me from sophomore year until he would become my husband. It was not an uncommon occurrence for me to fall asleep on the couch watching Disney movies in my parent's living room and he would sit there with me. He was patient in a way that was beyond his years.

On my 15th Birthday I had school and physical therapy. It wasn't exactly what most teenagers dream of doing on their birthday, but it wasn't out of the norm. Even though it wasn't perfect, my boyfriend wanted to make it special. So he picked me up from therapy and took me to his mom's house. He had made me a spaghetti dinner. I was feeling particularly under the weather, so I was not the most interesting of dinner dates, especially since I fell asleep after dinner while we watched TV until my curfew. And he loved me through it all.

One Sunday morning during my freshman year of college, I was attempting to get out of bed at home. When I tried to sit up, I heard an unsettling pop in my neck followed by pain that kept me from getting out of bed. I yelled for assistance from my mom who helped me slowly sit up. My neck had sharp pain that ran up into my ear. I couldn't turn my head and it felt best if I gave my head a little extra support from my hand. It wasn't bad enough to run to the hospital or anything, so I managed to slowly get ready and head to church. The pain didn't subside for a few days, so I decided to get it checked out. I often got ear infections, so I wanted to see if that was the culprit. I learned my lesson about waiting on these things when I had an ear infection a few years earlier that swelled my ear shut and kept me down for the count.

When I went to the doctor, he found that it wasn't my ear at all. The pain was coming from my neck and the pop I had heard was a muscle tearing. He wasn't sure why this would happen when I was just getting out of bed, but he did notice the muscles were all tensed up, so it was not healing. I was put on muscle relaxers until that healed. That didn't do any favors for my struggle with fatigue, but it did allow my neck to heal.

The pain became a very regular part of life. It seemed I was always injuring something and being sick seemed like the new norm. So I went from doctor to doctor attempting to get answers. This was always so discouraging. I would have vials and vials of blood taken just for everything to come back that I was healthy. I became so discouraged and frustrated from hearing that I was OK. I remember crying in the doctor's office every time I found out I didn't have what they were testing for. I know how backward this sounds, but I was battling an unknown enemy, which means I had no clear-cut plan of attack. Most of the focus began to be on pain management. I didn't want to load up on drugs so I just took a regular, high dose of prescription ibuprofen.

One orthopedic doctor finally determined it must just be depression and my pain was caused by "hyper-elastosis syndrome". I was tired, I was in pain, I was moody, so it must be depression. He put me on some antidepressants about a month before my wedding. I remember that those gave me the weirdest dreams, made me gain 40 pounds right before I had to squeeze into my wedding dress and worst of all, they made me feel numb. I wasn't happier, I wasn't more awake, and I still hurt, but I wasn't moody. I didn't like this but, I decided to put up with it for a little while.

After about a year, I was married, going to college part time and working part time at an antique mall. My prescription lapsed so I decided to get off those medicines cold turkey. This is absolutely the wrong way to go about working with antidepressants. I felt like I was on a boat. I was dizzy, tired, and queasy. These are things that should always be done under the supervision of a doctor.

Chapter Two: The Weight He Carried

"I take you Ali, to be my wedded wife to have and to hold, from this day forward, for better, for worse, for richer, for poorer, in sickness and in health, to love and to cherish, till death do us part, according to God's holy ordinance; and thereto I pledge thee my faithfulness." This is the promise that my husband made to me on December 30th, 2004. It was a year after high school and he was taking on the biggest challenge he could have imagined. The first few years he got the worse, the poorer, and the sickness. He stayed through all of it, all the while believing we would one day get our better, richer and healthier days.

I still had no diagnosis for what I was battling, and we were working opposite shifts. He would never know what he would be coming home to with my erratic moods and seldom feeling well. I would often be so mad at him that we would waste the time we did have together fighting. This was an ugly time in our marriage, but my husband stood by me. I believe that when someone has an invisible, undiagnosed or mental illness, it is just as much of a battle for those who love them. I didn't realize at the time how great of a gift my husband was. I didn't fully appreciate the fact that he put up with the anger and frustration that I often carried.

It was shortly after we got married that I found a doctor who was known for cracking the tough cases. I went to the initial consultation in her office and brought my husband along. He saw many things I didn't, so he was able to share those things with my doctor. The medical side was great to start working on, but the more helpful part of that visit was when she had us stop into the counselor's office. I talked to her about what I was dealing with and the unknowns. I had quite frankly become calloused to this way of life. However, when it was my husband's turn to share, this was eye opening. I hadn't realized the pain he had from my illness. The grief he had over not having natural children. The fear he carried over what was going on with the woman he loved and the looming terror that I could be taken from him by an unnamed enemy. That moment of seeing my husband vulnerable allowed me to take a step back and realize that having a chronic illness is in a way, harder on him than it was on me.

The next several months were spent going to the doctor every two weeks to find out what results came in from my bloodwork and investigating the next thing. My husband was with me at every one of these appointments, supporting me. I don't know how I would have gotten through this very frustrating season of my life without his support.

Sometime around six months to a year of going to the doctor, she noticed the circles on my scalp. I had psoriasis. She believed that what I was suffering from was psoriatic arthritis. I started a treatment plan for this and it worked pretty well. The pain was reduced, and my energy levels even started to go up a little, but the medicine had some risks that came with it. My immune system would be compromised, so I would catch everything, and the medication could build up on my retina and cause some problems. The issues were completely reversible if caught in time, so my doctor advised that I should go get my eyes checked once a year. They would look at my retina to make sure that a bull's eye pattern wasn't forming on it. This was a long annoying eye appointment every year. I had to look in a box and push a button every time I saw a red light. I had to go through the color blindness test and then I had to have my eyes dilated and they would look at my retina.

Every year was fine, until one year they asked me if I had any double vision. I told them, "Yeah but only when everyone does, like when you're tired or trying to watch TV laying down". That is when I learned that not everyone has double vision. That was a time in my life when I realized that my normal might not be what everyone else's normal was. Some things I was experiencing may be treatable if I realized that they are not just part of the human experience.

After lots of dizzying eye tests, they determined that I needed glasses that had prisms. When I got my first pair of these, it was life changing. Reading didn't exhaust my eyes; the words didn't move around on the page and I could watch TV even when I was tired. It also helped reduce some pesky headaches and a little of the fatigue that I always experienced. Best of all, it remedied my awful carsickness!

Chapter Three:

The D Word

After three or four years of our marriage, we had learned how to help reduce my pain, increase my energy level a bit and restore my ability to see clearly. I still found that even with the slight increase to my energy level, I was exhausted beyond belief and still very moody. I blamed my irrational mood swings on PMS and various other things and my husband took it like a champ.

When I had these mood swings, I felt like I was trapped in my own body. I could see myself being irrational, but I couldn't stop the spiral. We began to notice things like crowds, concerts and driving at night were miserable experiences that put me right into a high adrenalin panicked state. I figured I was "high strung" and just needed to work through it.

I also became obsessed with exercise. I knew I had to be strong and I used that as an excuse. I would find myself anxious and frustrated if I didn't get to work out. The irritation would manifest in a similar way as someone attempting to quit smoking. I would stay in that agitated state until I could get that workout in. I would work out injured and would even move plans around exercising. It was really starting to affect my life and even my relationship with my husband.

At one of my visits, I was referred to a new doctor at the office. I met with him and expressed some of my issues with fatigue, and he noticed that I was excessively emotional in the appointment. He started asking me some very pointed questions. By the nodding of his head as I would answer, I could tell I was falling into the criteria of something. I just didn't know what it was.

At the end of the list of questions he said I had major depression. I couldn't believe it. I was a Christian. I was seeking after God and I had major depression? I fell apart in the doctor's office. I felt like I failed. I had counselled others in the past. I was trained in different issues and struggles. So I thought I should be exempt from those types of things. As my husband heard the exact diagnosis that I did, he was not at all surprised by what he was hearing. He comforted me and reassured me that this was a good thing and that now we would be able to work toward getting better.

I knew that he always had my best interest at heart, so I took his word and went ahead and took the prescription. I had several follow up appointments to help me figure out the right dosage and found that a high dose allowed me to think clearly and it relieved me from the mood swings and loops of thoughts that interrupted everything. It also reduced the fatigue that I fought every day. This was a great answer and worked very well.

That doctor eventually moved on to his own practice and I began seeing my original doctor again. After seeing this doctor again for a few weeks, I ran out of my prescription and called for a refill. I was told she would not refill this prescription for me. This doctor felt that my depression should be able to be managed by leaning more into my faith. This of course was devastating for me. A medical doctor had reinforced the original feelings I had when I had been diagnosed. So, not only was I not feeling well, I was a bad Christian?

My husband of course was very frustrated. He loved me. He had seen me battle my own mind before and he had seen what I could be like when freed from that struggle and now we were back at square one. I decided that I was going to try the natural way of combatting my mental illness. I purchased a "happy light." This is a special lamp that mimics the effects of natural sunlight on the psyche. This did work surprisingly well. At this time in my life, I was working in an office buried deep in the bowels of the building and no natural light shined into my space. So I would use this special light every day for a couple hours. It helped trigger my mind to wake up and it would allow me to go to sleep at night. This didn't help the whole problem. I worked at memorizing Scripture and reading my Bible and doing studies for an hour or more a day. I tried a paleo diet and a healthy work out regiment. I also did my very best to consciously choose joy, think about my reactions and simply do better. I was basically faking my wellness.

My friends loved me and prayed me through these challenging times. They became used to my emotional responses, but my husband was the one who truly suffered. I was able to fake well all day, but once I got tired and night fall would happen, I would begin to have panic attacks for hours. I would shake and sweat while being cold and I would be so queasy, and I had no idea why.

I also found that my stomach was starting to give me many issues. I had heartburn with everything I ate and intestinal trouble for the first half of every day. I was once again beginning to feel the walls close in and once again I began feeling trapped in my own body. I felt like my world was spinning out of control and there was nothing that I could do to slow it down. I felt like I didn't have a voice or the words to express what I needed and how I felt.

Chapter Four

Comparing Notes

As I struggled through a wide variety of symptoms, I started con
notes with my family. My sister had developed similar symptoms ai.
did two of my cousins. We would talk and find that the odd, seemingly
unconnected symptoms were shared between the four of us. They all
had mood disorders, anxiety, stomach distress and pain. We all were in
a constant state of nursing some injury. Some of us had a more
aggravated variation of certain symptoms but, they were all still there.
My sister had several dislocations that resulted in several surgeries and
one of my cousins walked with a cane in her early 30's. So we all had
constant opportunities to talk with our doctors.

We would compare notes, sharing what medicines we had tried. We
would take that information back to our doctors and see what else we
could learn. We also started doing some research online and noticed we
fell into a disease called Elhers Danlos Syndrom. This was the disease
that my two "pen pals" from high school had. I was disqualified from
having this because my skin didn't stretch. It turns out there is a lot of
different symptoms to it, and different people have different variations
of the symptoms.

The short name for this condition is EDS. It is an incurable disease that
has a wide variety of symptoms. It effects the connective tissue in a
person. Everything from joint mobility, skin, internal organs and the
brain all have connective tissues holding them together and moving
messages throughout the body.

With this new information, we all went back to our doctors and shared
what we had found. Upon speaking with our various doctors, we
learned there was a specialist in just that condition in our area. So we
each made our appointment to meet her.

Chapter Five:

Beautiful

Bad News

Finally, my time on the waiting list was up and I was able to see the specialist. We talked through a variety of questions and I confirmed that each of these symptoms was present in my life. It was amazing that she was able to tell me exactly why each of the things I was experiencing was happening.

My anxiety was caused by connective tissues that were not protecting my nerves properly. Due to this I was more sensitive to loud noises and bright lights. Things like this would signal my body to release adrenaline and put me into a flight or fight mode. This was why I had so many panic attacks and anxiety.

I learned that because of this anxiety, my body was not processing my food right and that was causing the intestinal issues. The heartburn was due to my esophagus not sealing properly.

The pain I had and instability in my joints was caused by stretchy ligaments. This is what had allowed my joints so slowly stretch out of place. It also made me clumsy. The ligaments are the things that tell the body where it is in space. Without those in the proper place, your body isn't completely sure where the doorway or the desk are. This results in tripping over things and running into doorways.

I found out the extreme fatigue was due to the fact that my body can't get comfortable, so I don't get a good night sleep. Due to this very light sleep, dreams are vivid and can be remembered. This never lets me get into a good rem cycle.

I found out that this was a condition that had no cure. I would still live with these symptoms, but I now knew my enemy's name. I now knew who the adversary was that I was facing and I was now able to combat the various attacks it would make on me.

The doctor spent well over an hour with me and gave me additional resources to learn more about what I could do. She gave me a list of papers explaining the do's and don'ts of my diet and various supplements that would help curb the pain, even out my digestive issues and get me on a path to healing.

When I got to my car I cried. I cried not because I had an incurable condition that was going to cause pain and challenges in my life; not because I feared what this meant for my future. I cried because I was validated. There were years of going to doctors and being told that they didn't know what was going on. Years of them being skeptical as I told them my symptoms. Even some of my friends and acquaintances would doubt the things I was telling, because If you saw me walking down the street you would think I was a completely healthy young lady. If you checked my blood work and looked at my x-rays, you would also think I was healthy. But when we dug deeper and looked at the symptoms as a bigger picture, that is when the answers came.

I learned some new words that could describe my struggle. I had an invisible illness. This is an illness that makes me feel as sick as my 80-year grandmother, even though I look like a 30-year-old woman who has things together.

I was now a "spoonie". This is a person who must budget their day. There is a popular article in the chronically ill community that people refer to. It talks about the spoon analogy; this article compares the energy of a chronically ill person as being a currency of spoons. Everything that you do in a day, costs you a spoon. Taking a shower, going to the grocery store or working. When the spoons are gone, they are gone. I was able to use this analogy to better plan my life. If I knew that I wanted to go on a big weekend, I needed to keep the proceeding days simple, make sure I rest, and also anticipate the spend because it would take spoons from the days after also. It isn't the ideal life, but it is a life that I can manage.

Lastly, I learned I was a Zebra. A Zebra is a person who has the challenging condition of EDS. When you hear hoofbeats you think you hear a horse. You prepare for a horse and treat it as a horse, but what you hear isn't the fact. The fact is it is a Zebra. It is totally different from a horse and needs to be treated differently. When Zebras are born, they have a unique stripe pattern to them. No other Zebra has the same stripes. They are unique and different. Each person has a different manifestation of the EDS in their body, so we call ourselves Zebras.

Knowing these words helps me to find others who know the code. This allows us to share tips and trick on getting through everyday life. It allows us to empower one another and keep putting one foot in front of the other.

Chapter Six:

Managing My Illness

Now that I know its name, this was when the real battle began. I was sent home from my appointment with a couple sheets of paper and a whole lot of information. There were lists of supplements on there, and dietary changes that need to happen.

I went to the pharmacy and purchased the whole slew of bottles that held hope for a better future. I got myself a pill case with am and pm spots for every week and started sorting. It took some time to figure out what could sit on my stomach when, but I eventually got it down to an awkward science.

I had to add probiotics, acid reflux and allergy over the counter meds to the mix. So, my two arthritis pills a day grew to about eight in the morning and eight at night. I was OK with this. I had hope that this was going to be the life I had imagined. A life without the pain, heartburn and stomach issues that made travel so difficult. I had hope that the migraines that stole whole days from me would also be halted. It was worth the bother for me with no question.

On top of a pile of supplements, there were new foods to avoid. This was harder. I had to avoid foods that naturally aggravate the stomach and cause inflammation. The diet itself was challenging: Gluten free, dairy free, no artificial sugars and preservatives. I had to become one of those label reading types. This was hard. It was hard to say no to foods that I became so accustomed to for comfort or celebrations. It was farewell cake, goodbye ice cream, and see you later cheese. This was hard, but not nearly as hard as the grief and teasing from skeptical people who thought that it was a trend diet. It is nothing compared to the annoyance of trying to go to a restaurant and eat something besides salad, and (heaven forbid) someone attempt to cook for me.

It didn't take long to learn that this diet and these supplements did, in fact help. The pain was reducing, my stomach was recovering, and I was starting to have more energy. This was the positive life I was hoping for.

Though I was starting to feel better, I started to notice that the intense blues, the getting "hung up" on some thoughts and issues and anxiety just were not letting go. Driving at night was painful. It made my heart race every time an oncoming car had its lights on. Concerts and even church were tricky when they used the new lights for effects. I would spend time in the worship service with my eyes closed or looking down. I also found I still had those evening panic attacks and several panic moments when too many people were talking in the office or the phone was ringing too much.

I knew that the anxiety was triggered by signals misfiring due to a connective tissue problem, so this made it easier to go to my doctor and request a prescription for anxiety medicine. They started me on a very low dose in hopes that this would take the edge off my body's reaction to these artificial threats. Unfortunately, they didn't. I required a heavier dose than I ever hoped to need. It worked great during the day. I was able to get through the work day with little issue. However, once those wore off in the evening, it was back to the hours of panic attacks until I could finally fall asleep. I felt helpless and trapped. I can only imagine what it must have been like from my husbands' shoes. I worked with my doctor and found that if I took a low dose in the morning and a low dose in the evening, the panic attacks stopped. This was a tremendous relief.

I went along with this plan for several months and I notice I still had intense emotional hang ups. Things that should've been molehills to deal with, became mountains I couldn't see around.   I would worry excessively with no ability to listen to reason. I prayed, I read my Bible, had people pray with me, and confessed anything I thought it could be. Still the internal battle raged. I felt like I was a prisoner of my own mind. I didn't want anyone to know this struggle. I was embarrassed and thought it made me a bad Christian, so I attempted to hide it. I held it together as much as I could in public, but at home my husband had the struggle of watching me battle. He had the worry of the "what if" when he left me alone. My husband being the awesome man he is, didn't openly discuss our struggle but tried to fight on his own.

One day I went to the doctor feeling like I had a sinus infection. I had felt bad for several days and finally decided to see the doctor. The doctor looked in my ears, in my nose, throat and eyes. I was once again "fine". I was frustrated and in tears in the doctor's office, and she questioned if I was ok emotionally. I said of course I was and went home. I remember we had company over when I got to the house and I still could not pull it together. My husband thought I must have gotten terrible news, so he excused himself to a private room in the house to talk to me. When he found out it was because I was fine, he suggested that I tell my doctor about the previous antidepressant I was on.

In the moment, I dismissed his suggestion not wanting to admit that my brain was malfunctioning. The next day at work I was still off and remembering how ridiculous my reaction was, so I googled the medicine I used to be on. Lo and behold I was previously being treated for OCD. All the pieces slid together in that moment. The trap of the thoughts was OCD. I had thought OCD was straightening or cleaning. It can manifest in not being able to let go of a thought pattern or miss a work out.

I called my doctor and let her know, "I am not OK". I told her what I was once on and she got me right back on that medicine. We slowly increased the dose to where I once was. I remember when it started working, it was like someone tuned the picture all the way in and silenced the static. I felt like who I was, was finally free to come out. I felt mentally well.

Knowing the name of my enemy allowed me to put together a battle plan so that I had a chance of being successful.

Now that I'm feeling a little better and thinking much clearer, I am so thankful for my friends and family and especially my husband and all that they stood with me through. I think of the nights of frustration and tears that my husband spent out of my lack of control of my mind and am completely humbled and grateful beyond what I can ever express to him.

One of the keys to living well with a chronic illness is to have a solid faith in God. To trust that you are not alone, and your Creator can use even this confusing and less than ideal time to do something great for His kingdom.

Closely on the heels of this is having a solid support system. Having people to advocate for you, to help validate the symptoms and to take you to doctors and help push for the treatment and results you need. So often doctors are busy, and symptoms get dismissed. Having advocates and people to lock arms with can make a world of difference.

Chapter Seven: Shame in a Bottle

As a Christian woman who serves in church, I have gotten the opportunity to go to training for counseling and various ministries to people who are hurting deeply. This is a blessing and a curse. The more that I trained, the more I heard healthy people make light of medication. I also heard sermons preached on depression and heart issues that talk about the over prescribing of medication. This always made me hang my head in those services. I felt like all eyes were on me. As if they somehow knew.

I know that I did everything I could to get right with God and I know He met me where I was. Even though I knew that going without my medication was not going to be a positive thing, that it would make me less useful for God, I still felt shame.

I do want to go on record saying, the mind and the heart are tied to the spirit in such a mighty way. So often struggles with the mind, and emotional problems are due to a lack of trust in God or putting your hope in the wrong place or making idols over various things this world offers up to us. I also want to go on record saying, the brain is an organ. It is a product of a fallen world, and it too can be sick. There are many chemicals, and receivers in the brain that can have any number of problems. When these problems are present, that is when we need to partner closely with a medical doctor and get these things investigated. Not all of them are depression. Some can be sugar or hormones due to thyroid or various other things. These problems need to be found, diagnosed and treated by a true medical doctor. They should be monitored and supported by friends, family, and yes even your church and Small Group.

I want to see a church where people feel safe to say that they battle with mental illness. I would love to see a world where people can be open that they take medication to regulate how the brain is firing. When we get to this place, the church will have permission to speak into our lives and help us stay healthy spiritually. It is so easy to use your medication as a crutch. So it is good to have someone keep you in check and say, "I think that you still have a sin in this area and I think that is what is causing your current rut." When that happens, people with mental illness can live a powerful life and be a genuine threat to Satan himself.

In today's world there is no shortage on discussion about mental illness, depression and the things that they cause. People are talking about that possibly being the cause of the mass shootings or the epidemic of suicide and drug use. I think it is important for the church to join in on this conversation. It is time for the church to lock arms and walk along with people struggling and show the healing power of our Great Physician to a world that is desperately sick.

I do think if this were to happen, and revival was to sweep the nation, that the number of these prescriptions would go down. But I don't think they would go away. Just like I don't think heart disease or diabetes, or arthritis will go away with revival. I do think that the people who are trying to numb where the spirit can work with medication, would find a vibrant life with Christ, able to enjoy all the hills and valleys of life.

One final note I want to make on this topic is when you get that perfect balance of spiritual support, medical support, diet and exercise you will feel good, possibly great. I have from time to time thought I was in remission or healed and decided to stop taking my medicine. This is always a bad idea without a doctor walking this journey with you. I have found every time that I make this mistake, (and yes, I have repeated it), that it is the medication and the balance keeping me going. I have learned I need to accept, I am sick, my body is sick, my mind is sick and the only way I can feel well is to follow the doctor's instructions. I encourage you to stay the course of your treatment, and if you are the loved one walking the journey, gently remind your loved one to stay the course.

THANK YOU

Thank you for taking the time to read my story about how I learned I was a Zebra. Thank you for taking the time to listen to what I learned and how my family rallied around me. I really hope that if you are in this same battle that you keep putting one foot in front of the other and pressing for answers. I also hope that if you know your enemy, fight it well, keep firm in your faith and surround yourself with a solid support system.

Check out my other published titles found on Amazon

Journey to Healing

This book walks through the hardest years of my life and shares how God led me to healing, and further growth in my relationship with Him. This book also has many practical steps on how to get through the grieving process and help others around you who are grieving.

Poetry Through the Psalms Series

These books are written to help you learn a fresh new way of worship as I share my own intimate walk through the Psalms using poetry. It was so great to write these books. It is my hope that you will also find a new appreciation for the Psalms.

Back to Work Again – Bouncing Back After Job Loss

A very practical book about finding a job in today's world of social media and online applications. I wrote this book after I had spent eight years at a job that I loved. After we were acquired by a competitor, I found myself looking for a job. Searching for a job was very different this time around, and I wanted to share some of the tips and tricks I found helpful on my own job search.

My Little Country Life Series

This is a light-hearted series from the view of child growing up in the country. Life is simple, yet adventures are never in shortage.

Centrifugal Force

This is my story. I lay it all on the line, the good, the bad, the ugly and the gut wrenching. I have battled through chronic illness, a young marriage, the adoption system and a wild ride with a child I loved as my very own. Through this story you will see God's mighty hand move even when it seems life has not been fair. It is through some of life's most painful happenings that God moves in the most amazing ways.

Check Out

Books by Alise Gilley on Facebook to see when new releases are coming.

My Author Profile on Amazon

And my blog: https://alisegilley.wixsite.com/website

Printed in Great Britain
by Amazon

26674343R00020